The Parent's 20 Minute Guide

A guide for parents about how to help their
children change their substance use

 center for motivation & change

2014

First Printing: 2013

ISBN 978-1-304-67590-3

Center for Motivation & Change

276 Fifth Avenue Suite 1101

New York, NY 10001

www.motivationandchange.com

Contents

WELCOME

Parenting* is hard. If you are reading this, you are likely a very concerned parent who is looking for guidance about how to help your child who is using substances (or engaging in other risky behaviors). You may have mild concerns about your child's focus at school, choice of friends, new "minimalist" communication style with you, or you may be facing sudden and terrifying changes. Whatever your particular mix of worries as a parent, your child's drug use (including alcohol) tends to make it that much more nerve-racking—sometimes explosive.

> ***A note to grandparents, aunts, uncles, and foster and adoptive parents and other caregivers: please understand "parent" as shorthand and feel no less welcome here.**

A Complex Problem for your Child

The factors that go into the decision to use substances are complex for everyone, and teenagers and young adults are at a particular disadvantage because their brains are not yet fully developed. With their immature prefrontal cortexes, it is normal for adolescents to struggle with impulsivity and decision making, and their notoriously fluctuating or "raging" hormones further destabilize the situation. The addition of mood altering substances at this stage of development is especially problematic as they directly impact teenagers' brains which are growing and learning. These substances alter their moods and decisions, the way they feel, think, and act and to that end, what they learn about themselves and the world around them.

Many teens who decide to start using substances early also struggle with psychiatric problems like depression, bipolar disorder, anxiety problems, ADHD, conduct disorder, or early onset psychotic disorders. Many have learning disorders and academic problems, or impulse control problems that lead to relationship, legal, institutional, or authority problems. In addition, teens are particularly sensitive to peer dynamics (including making/ending friendships, sexual identity issues, bullying, etc.) and to stressful situations like their parents' marital status or someone they're close to dying. There's a lot in the mix at this stage of life!

A Complex Problem for You

It's complicated for you as well! If your child is struggling with a substance use problem, you face the reactions of school staff, police, other parents, and extended family members: often including judgment, misunderstanding, punishment, fear, and "help" that can feel overbearing and shake your confidence as a parent. And not least of all, cooperation and collaboration with your co-parent can be seriously tested under this stress.

But you *can* help. And we hope you keep reading.

The CRAFT of Helping

There is a new way to help a loved one with substance problems, called CRAFT (Community Reinforcement and Family Training). CRAFT is a scientifically proven set of tools and strategies for any family member or friend who wants to help. Developed by Robert Meyers at the University of New Mexico, the CRAFT approach targets motivation and behavior to help you, your child, and your whole family. It is the leading research-supported way for families to help their substance using loved ones. Family members who are trained in CRAFT are more likely (than those trained to do interventions or who attend Al-Anon) to reduce or stop substance use in their loved one as well as increase the loved one's willingness to get help. In CRAFT, the concerned family member (that's you!) also feels better.

How to Use This Guide

Unlike other approaches, CRAFT teaches you how to stay involved in a *positive, ongoing* way, while also taking care of yourself. This guide will help you with such tools as:

- How to react when your child has been using substances and when he has NOT been using substances

- How to co-parent and collaborate as effectively and smoothly as possible

- Getting more of what you want to see from your child and less of what you don't

- How to talk to your child so that you are more likely to be heard

- How to take care of yourself all along the way

For each topic, we explain why it's important and how to use it to encourage change. We provide worksheets with examples to show you how CRAFT strategies look in action. We encourage you to use these worksheets to practice the skills as many times as you want or need. Feel free to skip around—it's not necessary to go through the topics in order, but it is important to practice each one.

> **<u>Last Things First</u>:**
>
> **It's so important to practice that we want to emphasize it now, before we tell you what it is you'll be practicing. Practice, practice, practice, and have patience with yourself as you do. Some or all of the following skills may be new to you. Some may be the opposite of what you have been trying to do (confronting, lecturing, punishing). Learning to do it differently requires practice and patience. You won't get it right every time, and that's okay, that's part of the process. Give yourself room to make mistakes, and try not to get discouraged. Keep practicing—but don't push yourself too hard. Try short stints each day and get some rest in between. In other words, try out these ideas for 20 minutes a day!**

We wrote this short guide to address parenting issues that wouldn't fit in the book we wrote for everybody (spouses, adult children, friends etc.), *Beyond Addiction: How Science and Kindness Help People Change.* (That book is for you too, with much more about the nature of substance problems, the science of change, treatment options for your loved one, and CRAFT strategies.)

We hope this is the beginning of positive change for you and your family. We appreciate the effort it takes to be a force for good. Thank you, truly. Take care of yourself, communicate, learn the CRAFT behavioral strategies, practice—and trust that things will change. Forty years of research and all our clinical experience says they will.

We start with the topic of problem solving because that's what you are facing! Your child's substance use, as well as the ensuing problems with communication, behavior, friend choices, school performance, and emotional development (you name it!). We will discuss all of these issues, but as we start this process we want you to have a general strategy for approaching ANY problem.

CRAFT (among other behavioral approaches) sets out seven steps for solving problems.* This approach will take you beyond painful avoidance strategies and unreliable quick fixes to help you work through problems thoroughly and systematically. As you practice with these steps, try to apply (and give yourself credit for) what you already do well, and take the time you need to learn what would be useful that you don't already know.

1

Define the problem as narrowly as you can.

Often what people take as "the problem" is actually many smaller problems lumped together. No wonder they feel overwhelmed. When you describe a problem, be on the lookout for multiple problems embedded within your description, and tease them apart. The idea is to tackle one relatively discrete problem at a time. Solutions are more manageable with a series of smaller problems and you'll feel more accomplished and optimistic as you get through each one.

2

Brainstorm possible solutions.

In this step, your task is to write down as many solutions as you can think of, to foster a sense of possibility and give yourself some choice. Brainstorming is an open, free-for-all process of allowing every idea in the door as they come, to be sorted and refined later. Your inner critic will tend to dismiss ideas out of habit or fear; but some of these could be viable options if you gave them a chance. List without judging. Try not to rule out anything before you've written down every conceivable solution to your problem.

---

*   Adapted from pp.187-190 in: Smith, J., & Myers, R. (2004). *Motivating substance abusers to enter treatment: working with family members.* New York: Guilford Press.

3

Eliminate unwanted ideas.

Now that you have an exhaustive list of potential solutions, you can examine them more closely and cross out any that are unappealing. Eliminate options that you can't actually imagine ever doing, have too many downsides, or seem unrealistic. If you end up crossing off every idea, then return to step 2 and brainstorm again.

4

Select one potential solution or goal.

Pick one solution that seems doable to you, that you can see yourself trying this week. Hint: a doable goal is put in brief, simple, and positive terms (what you will do, not what you won't do or haven't been doing), is specific and measurable, reasonable and achievable, in your control, and involves skills you already have or are learning. (For a detailed discussion of goal setting, see Chapter 8 of our book, *Beyond Addiction*.)

5

Identify possible obstacles.

Next, identify potential obstacles that could get in the way of completing your task. By anticipating problems you can plan strategies for dealing with them. This can include specific, predictable obstacles as well as a more general awareness that unforeseen challenges may arise, which can lend you some emotional resilience in dealing with them.

6

Address each obstacle.

Design specific strategies to cope with each obstacle. Not just, "I'm sure I can deal with it," but exactly how you will get past it and move forward.

7

See how things go.

After you've carried out your plan, evaluate the process... How did it go? Look at what went well and what was more challenging in the implementation. Did your strategies for dealing with obstacles work well? Did obstacles come up that you hadn't predicted? Is there anything you would do differently next time? This is how you figure out what works and what doesn't work for you.

3. PRACTICE, PRACTICE, PRACTICE! YOU CAN'T GET IT RIGHT EVERY TIME

As you read this guide you may think, "but I've tried this before and it didn't work." Maybe so, but perhaps you have not combined the consistency, timing, collaboration, and persistence that gets results.

Taking part in this change process means you're learning too. Take pride when something goes better because of an effort you made to change, and be kind to yourself and patient with your child when it doesn't. Learning any new thing takes practice, whether it's positive communication, golf, cooperating with your spouse, or figuring out your new phone. At first, most of us feel awkward, even "bad at it." As you practice with CRAFT, you might get frustrated and be tempted to give up. You might say to yourself, "this isn't working," "this isn't me," or "I can't do this, and my kid doesn't care anyway." Such thoughts and impulses are normal when you're learning; that is, they are *part of the process*, not reason to quit.

As in all learning, *wanting* to know the skill doesn't get you the skill; practice does. Practice again and again. Experiment and learn from the data you collect, and adjust your plans accordingly. Track your practice to create a record you can look back on, to help you remember what you're doing, when you're doing it, and how it's actually going—which might be different from how it feels like it's going on a bad day. (*Beyond Addiction* the book includes a number of specific tracking exercises, which you can find on the *Beyond Addiction* website at www.beyondaddictionbook.com.) By tracking you can make connections between your effort and its effects on the wellbeing of your child, your family, and yourself.

Developing your helping skills will take time and patience. Helping your child change through your relationship will be a process. Give yourself room to practice, make mistakes, and not get discouraged. You will get better at the changes you are trying to make, and so will your child.

Beyond Addiction: How Science and Kindness Help People Change (A Guide for Families) is available from Scribner in bookstores online and near you.

TAKING CARE OF YOURSELF

We put "taking care of yourself" front and center in this guide because it is critically important to helping effectively and helping for the long term. Having a child struggling with substance use is incredibly stressful, and has the capacity to wear everyone down, losing your patience, balance, and resilience.

In this section, we focus on three important aspects of taking care of yourself: 1) understanding the stress of this situation and developing concrete ways to relieve that stress, 2) being aware of your emotional states, in particular your very natural negative emotions, and learning to effectively manage them, and 3) finding ways to get support and avoid isolation.

This section includes three topics:

1
This Is Really Stressful!

This Is Really Stressful! Worksheet

2
Manage Your Emotions

Manage Your Emotions Worksheet

3
You're Not Alone

You're Not Alone Worksheet

1. THIS IS REALLY STRESSFUL!

If you love someone with a substance use problem, worry, frustration, and feelings of helplessness probably consume large amounts of your time and energy. Even more so if that someone is your child. As you focus on your child, taking care of yourself probably falls to the bottom of your list, if it makes the list at all. You might reason that you'll feel better when your child gets better, so it makes sense to prioritize his needs at your (and perhaps the rest of the family's) expense for now. This impulse to suspend paying attention to your own health and happiness is understandable but is likely to cause more problems than you realize if it causes you to be reactive, anxious, or easily frustrated. Your child is struggling with a variety of issues (all in the spirit of growing up!) and he needs you to be strong, calm, and optimistic. It helps if you are sleeping, eating well, and finding some comfort and joy in your life. It helps if you don't hang your wellbeing on his. Having your health and outlook on life be dependent on the choices your child makes can be too much for a child—even an adult child—to bear.

Taking care of yourself is vital to helping your child and the rest of your family. Try to resist the impulse to put your life on hold and live only in emergency/panic mode. How can you possibly go to a movie when you're worried that your child is out getting high again?! Well, what if taking a break from worrying is the most helpful thing you could do right now, *and you can learn how?*

Remember the safety announcement on planes before takeoff: secure your own oxygen mask first before you help someone else. This is for the benefit of the whole group. Helping works the same way on the ground. You need a certain amount of "oxygen" (sleep, nutrition, exercise, socializing, and fun) to sustain you as you help your child. Without attention to your own needs, you risk collapsing before you manage to help. Even if you stay standing, you won't be able to think, plan, act, and troubleshoot as effectively—as you can when you're healthy, optimistic, and resilient. The strategies suggested in the CRAFT approach require that you approach problems with clarity and consistency, which is nearly impossible to do if you are physically or emotionally exhausted.

What is Resilience?

Resilience is how you "roll with" life, or how you adapt to change and what flexibility and creativity you can muster for solving problems. And it is the point of self-care and is absolutely required in raising a teenager. Without resilience, over time, you become less able to take an emotional "hit" from your child without sinking into despair or lashing back with anger. As you try to help your child change, tension with your child will likely rise (as they disagree, as they struggle to change, etc.). If you react to that tension with high emotion (anger, despair, panic), it will make it harder for you to be an effective helper and make your child more resistant to being helped.

Depending on the severity of your situation, you may not feel like there's room for anything other than reacting to the latest crisis. We encourage you to look at it another way - you can't afford *not* to take care of yourself, because sometimes people change "overnight," but usually it takes longer. Even when there's an Ah-Ha moment, the real work of sustaining change is ongoing (if you've ever made a New Year's resolution, you know this). So, helping your child change her relationship to substances will likely be a long-term project that's better approached as a marathon rather than a sprint. You'll need to keep up your energy reserves and pace yourself. You'll need to prepare for hills, weather, and competition. Even if your situation improves fairly quickly—and we hope it does—you'll be more helpful if you bring your best self to it. It's not "touchy-feely" to take care of yourself; it's tactical.

THIS IS REALLY STRESSFUL! WORKSHEET

 Suffocating from worry, fear, anger, resentment, or stress will not help you help someone else. You need "oxygen" *continuously* to be the best support possible for your child. We recommend that you spend time *each week* doing something that makes you feel good, relaxed, content, and soothed—something you want to do as opposed to something you think you should do.

How will you contribute to your own self-care this week? Consider your health (nutrition, sleep, exercise) as well as what nourishes you intellectually, emotionally, and spiritually. In case it's been so long since you've entertained the notion of doing what you'd like to do that you've forgotten, we've included a list of possibilities at the end of this worksheet.

Step 1: Identify areas of your life that need attention, where a change would help you feel less stressed or improve the overall quality of your life. The following questions may help you think about this:

- How do you feel about your <u>intellectual wellbeing</u>? (Have you felt cut off or disengaged from matters that used to interest you? When was the last time you learned something new? Had a discussion about something other than your child?)

- How do you feel about your <u>physical health</u>? (How are you sleeping? When was the last time you exercised? Have you found yourself eating poorly? When was the last time you had a check-up?)

- How do you feel about your <u>emotional wellbeing</u>? (Have you been more emotionally reactive lately (short fuse, quick to cry etc.)? Do you find that you are feeling numb, shut down, angry? Are you doing or saying things that don't match who you want to be?)

- How do you feel about <u>your own use of substances</u>? (We're not saying that using any substances on your part is necessarily problematic for your child, but it will have an impact—along with everything else you do. Practically, your child may feel permitted or even invited by the presence and availability of substances. Emotionally, he will learn the reasons you use substances: this is how you pick yourself up, knock yourself out, handle the pressure, or blow off steam. Would change on your part help support change on his?)

Step 2: Pick an area (from above) and brainstorm possible solutions: what you'd like to accomplish related to your self-care and why it would help you build the resiliency you need to help your child.

What I would like to accomplish...	Why it would help me...
I would like to sleep through the night.	It would help me feel less irritable in the morning, when we often fight.
I would like to find the time to read a good book.	It would help me take a break and feel less resentful about spending all my time worrying about my child.
Your ideas:	

Steps 3: Select (e.g., by process of elimination or because they jump out at you) two solutions and convert them into doable goals (remember: keep them brief, simple, positive, specific and measurable, reasonable and achievable, in your control, and involving skills you already have or are learning). Set two self-care goals for the coming week. We recommend at least one of them be something that's entirely enjoyable to you.

To improve my self-care, this week I will: _____

_____

Example: *I will go for a run 2 times this week to blow off steam and feel more tired when I go to bed. This will help me sleep better.*

To increase joy in my life, I will: _____

_____

Example: *I will go to the bookstore on my way home from work and buy a new book. Then I will stop doing chores at 10:00 and get lost in my book.*

Step 4: Identify obstacles that could interfere with your "goals of the week."

Obstacles to Practicing this Goal	Coping Skills for Handling Obstacles
It's hard to find time to go for a run.	Plan out the week and schedule time for runs around other activities. Commit to it like an appointment.
I'm too worried to sit and read. I get distracted.	Take deep breaths and give myself permission to start small. If I can read for 15 minutes, that's better than no break at all.

There are many ways to tend to your mind, body, heart, and soul. We include this by-no-means complete list to help you brainstorm your way to better self-care.

- Visit with a friend (face-to-face, on the phone, by email, etc.).

- Cook your favorite meal.

- Go out to eat your favorite meal or eat a "comfort food" that you find soothing.

- Take a class in a topic that interests you.

- Let yourself space out and watch TV.

- Go to a movie.

- Watch hilarious videos on YouTube.

- Get a manicure, pedicure, or massage.

- Go for a walk or run. Let yourself take in the sounds and smells. Try to be present.

- Go for a hike (even in the city). Walk somewhere you have never been before. Take in the "newness" of your surroundings.

- Engage in a sport (either alone or with people) that you enjoy (swimming, golf, biking, tennis, yoga, basketball, bowling...).

- Do an activity that gets your adrenaline pumping (rock climbing, skydiving, roller coasters, horseback riding, karaoke singing).

- Take a nap; let yourself doze off.

- Sincerely compliment or appreciate another person (this could be a stranger).

- Play cards, do brain teasers, crosswords, word games.

- Listen to music you enjoy.

- Get a haircut.

- Help someone out.

- Take your dog for a walk; play with a pet.

- Sit outside and watch the clouds for ten minutes; sit in a park and watch the birds and squirrels.

- Watch a live sporting event or go hear some live music.

- Visit an exhibit at a museum or wander around a gallery.

- Go for a drive.

- Lift weights, take a class at the gym, hire a trainer for a few sessions.

- Listen to a podcast.

- Go to a bookstore or magazine store. Read something for pleasure.

- Go to services at your usual place of worship.

- Go to services not at your usual place of worship.

- Give time to a hobby you enjoy (photography, knitting, gardening, cooking, painting…).

- Meditate; download a guided mindfulness training.

- Buy your favorite flowers; don't forget to smell them.

- Re-read a favorite book, poem, or article. Sit and flip through a magazine.

- Draw a picture; doodle.

- Spend an hour window-shopping; visit a flea market.

- Drink a cup of tea or coffee while doing nothing else.

- Volunteer for an afternoon or evening.

- Take a bath; light your favorite candle.

- Write yourself a nice note that you can read again and again.

- Make a photo album.

- Do a puzzle.

- Take a day trip; plan a trip.

- Play an instrument; learn a new song.

- Dress in your favorite outfit; buy yourself something you have wanted to wear.

- Visit your favorite coffee shop.

- Buy yourself an ice cream cone.

For more ideas and a thorough self-care assessment, see the self-care chapters of our book, *Beyond Addiction*, especially the "You Are Here" exercise.

2. MANAGE YOUR EMOTIONS

Do you know the expression, "You're only as happy as your unhappiest child?" While we wish it were not true, many parents feel exactly this way when their child is struggling (with substance use or any other behavioral/emotional problem). Instead of feeling the joy of watching a child grow up and experience life, they are awash in a variety of painful, negative feelings. You may find yourself yelling and even screaming, nagging, begging, crying, or just shutting down. At times, you may feel like giving up completely.

Two things about these feelings: 1) They are normal, and 2) you weren't born knowing how to deal with the situation you are facing, but you can learn. Managing these negative feelings is an important job to take on as they needn't prevent you from helping your child or enjoying yourself, the rest of your family, and the other parts of your life.

Your Negative Emotions

When your child is using substances or engaging in other risky behaviors, you will naturally feel afraid, angry, betrayed, ashamed, confused, guilty, and a host of other painful emotions. Your task is manage them so you don't act on them with your child.

Acknowledging your feelings to yourself as they happen helps defuse them, though it may seem counter intuitive. Just the act of being aware can help keep your negative emotions from bursting out of you in the form of confrontational or hostile behaviors that push away your child and take you further from your ultimate goals. Awareness gives you choice and helps you change course to be most effective. If you know you are about ready to boil over, you can step back and decide to finish a conversation in the morning when cooler heads prevail. If you know you are on the verge of panic, you can ask a loved one or friend for support. Oftentimes, letting your negative feelings simply *be* allows them to pass, as they do when you don't fan the flames or act on them, giving you quicker access to the positive emotions you need to help your child change. (Remember why you're reading this in the first place: you *love* this kid. That's where help comes from.)

The Impact of Emotions on Your Behavior

Acting on your emotions by breaking down, confronting, or detaching is counter-productive in many ways. Let us count them: 1) you ultimately feel worse (for losing control, for saying things you regret); 2) you help your child divert attention from their actions by making you the problem ("my mom's crazy," "she always overreacts"); 3) your child may cope with the negative feelings brought on by the situation by turning to substances more (this is *not* to blame you for your child's behavior, but to help you do everything you can to remove yourself as her excuse); 4) a truth about motivation: confrontation leads to resistance and your child's motivation is likely to drop; and 5) as your relationship deteriorates due to conflict or detachment, so does your positive influence.

The alternative to acting on your negative feelings is to manage them and find ways to be calm and non-confrontational. Engaging with your child in this way does not mean you are passively accepting risky behavior; it means your child will more likely hear what you think about the behavior and, more important, about healthier ways to behave. Staying connected in a calmer way also lets her know you care (whatever she says in the heat of the moment, trust that she cares that you care) and are prepared to stay the course. Not least, you will be modeling the behavior you want to see from your child.

Easier said than done, right?

How to Manage

- Take care of yourself. Do at least the minimum to keep up your resilience—enough sleep, a balanced diet, exercise, and so on—and then some: time to yourself, activities you enjoy, time with people who make you laugh and feel loved, and so on.

- Anticipate your negative emotions. How does your child push your buttons? What triggers your anger, yelling, and other unproductive behaviors? Make a list; then read on to learn some other ways to respond.

- In your head, label your feelings and describe to yourself what's happening: "I feel really angry incredibly fast when he uses that disrespectful tone with me." Just narrating to yourself what's happening can provide a little bit of distance between you and your emotional reaction.

- Take a "time out." Give yourself permission to avoid the most triggering situations while you try to improve the climate in your home.

- Imagine it was your neighbor's kid or your nephew/niece. How would you react? Perhaps somewhat less judgmentally and more calmly. Try on this perspective for a couple of minutes and see if it helps you get through the moment.

- Set a limit. If, upon reflection, you choose not to put up with a particular behavior (such as name-calling or swearing, yelling or physical aggression), plan what the consequences will be and use the communication skills in this guide and in our book, *Beyond Addiction*, to explain this to your child in advance. In a calm moment, you might say, "I know it's hard for you to keep your voice down when you're mad, but if you yell at me again, you will lose your computer for the night."

> **Remember your goals:** You want your child to change her relationship with substances and you want her to eventually make the changes for reasons that matter to her. You want her to feel lovable, loved and supported, because no matter how scared, angry, or frustrated you get, this is your child and you love her.

MANAGE YOUR EMOTIONS: WORKSHEET

 This exercise will help you recognize what triggers your negative emotions and behaviors, so you can be ready with a more helpful—or at least non-harmful—response. In the left-hand column, list everything you can think of that your child does that pushes your buttons and makes you more likely to act on your negative emotions. Then, in the right-hand column, plan an alternative coping response. Choose one coping response to practice this week.

Trigger	Coping Response
He comes home obviously under the influence.	This week, I will practice resisting the urge to talk to him when he comes home under the influence; instead, I will go to a place in our home where I don't see him and where I can focus on something else.
He ignores me/takes a really snotty tone with me when I ask how his day went.	This week, I will go in my room, relax, and tell myself I can talk to him more effectively tomorrow when I'm calmer.
Your ideas:	

3. YOU'RE NOT ALONE: REDUCING ISOLATION

You may wonder if anyone can really understand what you're going through. The truth *is* that your path is unique. Some of what happens could only happen in your family. Yet millions of people have walked down similar roads; roads with stories, realizations, experiences, heartbreaks, and successes that look, sound, and feel a lot like what you're going through.

We recommend talking to some of these people. Research has found time and again that social support helps when it comes to, well, pretty much everything. You may worry about privacy, gossip, and the "public" perception of your child/yourself/your family. You might not consciously choose to withdraw; you may simply be rushing around with your heart in your throat, and your focus has naturally turned inward. You may feel protective of your child; frankly, at times, embarrassed. These feelings can easily lead you to pull away from the support systems you normally rely on. Or you may not be in the habit of asking for help. You may even be dead-set against it.

While these are reasonable concerns and valid feelings, isolation can make you feel worse over time, depriving you of the energy and resiliency you need to cope—and to help. Do not underestimate the toll that isolation can take. It can exacerbate depression, anxiety, and stress, making it more difficult for you to handle hard, emotionally charged situations. Over time, your buffer zone (or emotional resilience) gets smaller and smaller; your ability to take an emotional "hit" from your child, be it small (late for school), medium (truancy notice from school) or large (crashed the car) without sinking or reacting badly yourself gets really diminished.

Conversely, social support can increase your resilience. You are not alone, but isolation can creep up on you. Fighting the pull toward isolation will help you feel better, and help you help better.

How could you connect with another person or people this week? Keep in mind, support has many faces and you may have different needs at different times. Consider who in your life might be useful to confide in, but also who is good at having fun, making you laugh, distracting you, or helping you relax. Reaching out to others doesn't have to mean pouring out your heart (though if that is what you need right now, go for it). Taking time out from your problems is as important as talking them through.

Even if you don't feel like isolation is a big factor right now, try to do something social at least once a week to see if it helps. "Something social" can be as simple as a phone chat with your sister or as elaborate as a dinner with friends.

Step 1: Identify people in your life who fill different needs for you.
(Some people may fit in more than one category.)

Good Listener:	
Good Advice Giver:	
Just for Fun/ Makes Me Laugh:	
Cheerleader/ Encourages Me:	
Confidant:	
Playmate/Likes to Do Things with Me:	
Shoulder to Cry On:	

Step 2: Look over your answers to Step 1 and pick a person you'd like to see this week. Think about what kind of socializing you'd most prefer right now—who and why. Then brainstorm how you could connect with the person this coming week.

I need someone who is: _____

I want to spend time with: _____

I would like to do*: _____

---

*   For this line include specifics like when you would like to meet the person and what you would like to do with him or her.

Step 3: Identify obstacles that could interfere with meeting your goal(s) for connecting with others this week. Then, come up with a strategy to address each one of these barriers and maximize your chances of accomplishing your goal.

Obstacles to achieving my goal	Coping strategy for dealing with the obstacles
It's hard to find time.	Ask for help with household chores to free up some time during the evenings. Schedule a "date" in advance so that we have it on the calendar.
My friend might not be available.	Have a back-up plan in case she's not free. Call her a week in advance so that she has a better chance of making herself available.

COMMUNICATING

As you well know, communication breaks down in the face of stress and high emotion. Therefore, developing new communication strategies may be the most powerful thing you can do to improve your situation and help your child. Good communication is crucial in creating space for change to take place, and it can effectively tip the motivational seesaw towards it. More than that, developing your communication skills will help you feel more understood, listened to, and better in ALL the relationships in which you practice them. You might feel tempted to jump ahead to the "Helping" section, feeling understandably anxious to see changes in your child's behavior and start doing what you can as quickly as possible... We urge you, however, to not skip over this communication section because so many of the active strategies of CRAFT that come later truly rely on good, effective communication to have the impact you want, which is why we have purposefully put communication first in the order.

Our topics in this communication section include how to listen more effectively, how to offer feedback and information, and how to make requests most constructively, with the least amount of argumentation or defensiveness. We also discuss the importance of validation and empathy throughout communication, and how to stay out of conversational "traps." But we begin with the overarching goal: keeping a connection and sense of positive forward movement through a communication. We think of this as keeping track of whether the traffic lights (of communication) are red or green.

This section includes six topics:

1. Pay Attention to the Traffic Lights!

2. Communicate with LOVE: Listening
   Listening Worksheet

3. Communicate with LOVE: Offering Information
   Offering Information Worksheet

4. Communicate with LOVE: Validating and Empathizing

5. The Seven Elements of Positive Communication
   Positive Communication Worksheet

6. Avoiding Conversational Traps

1. PAY ATTENTION TO THE LIGHTS!

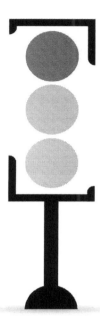

Good communication starts with this overarching goal: to stay connected and keep moving forward. You have, no doubt, already tried to talk to your child (or shout at, plead with, etc.) about changing her behavior. We'd guess you have started many a conversation with great intentions only to see her go off course and become unproductive or downright destructive.

Imagine if there were traffic signals in conversation to tell you when to stop or go; to help you get safely to your destination. Actually, if you know what to look for, there are:

The light is **green** when your child is positively engaged with you, willing to listen and respond constructively, and maybe, though not necessarily, talking about change.

The light is **red** when your child is destructively engaged with you (yelling, cursing, going silent), not listening, and probably moving away from the idea of change. For example, when she is defending her use of substances.

That may sound obvious, but when you *pay attention* to these lights and respond accordingly, you are much more likely to get somewhere and avoid harm along the way. Here are some examples:

You: "I'd like to talk to you about not drinking at the party tonight."

Your child:

Green Lights	Red Lights
"Okay, but can we not have a fight about it?"	**"You're just going to force your rules on me."**
"Can I tell you what I think?"	**"Why do you always overreact?"**
"I won't drink, I have practice early in the morning."	**"I hate when you interfere with my social life."**

Red lights are frustrating, especially when you're in a rush to see change. You may be tempted to "gun it" and try to force your way through. But you know from experience that ignoring red lights is dangerous: people end up fighting, saying things they regret, feeling worse instead of better, and no closer to positive change—in fact, often further from it.

Paying attention to the lights will help you stay oriented to the goal of communication: you want it to go forward. You don't want to crash.

What follows are strategies and approaches to communicating that will allow for more green lights than red, as well as ways to notice those red lights, so you can stop and try again.

> **A Side Note:** Take a moment to notice Red and Green lights in conversation with anyone. When you don't jump to taking a side, you will find people consider both sides more easily. When you strongly advocate for only one side, notice how quickly the other person picks up the opposite side of the argument.

2. COMMUNICATING WITH LOVE: LISTENING

You've probably heard it said that love is not a noun; it's a verb. According to an acronym that helps people remember communication skills, LOVE is *four* verbs: **Listening**, **Offering**, **Validating,** and **Empathizing**. You'll hit more green lights when you communicate with LOVE.

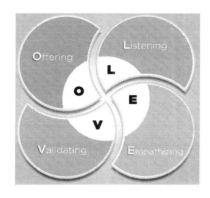

Listening

There are many ways to listen to another person, some more helpful than others. A powerful therapeutic approach called Motivational Interviewing emphasizes four strategies: open-ended questioning, affirming, reflecting or active listening, and summarizing.   It's an approach to listening that helps the red lights turn green, instead of driving straight through and hoping for the best.

1. Open-ended questions – These are questions that call for some elaboration, that can't be answered with one word (e.g. *"What concerns you most?" "What would you like to be different?").* Open questions invite description, giving you, the listener, more to listen to and learn from. They also set a collaborative tone, as they communicate more interest in your child's view. Open-ended questions should be inviting information (from them), not suggesting information (from you).

Closed question	Open-ended question
"Are you mad at your teacher for calling us?"	*"What is your reaction to your teacher calling us?"*
"Do you think you shouldn't have a curfew?"	*"What about this curfew do you think isn't fair?"*

2. Affirmations – Listen for the positives. Communication can easily become all about what's wrong. Noticing what's going right and explicitly acknowledging it can change everything: it puts some balance back in the conversation, holds a positive connection, and keeps you headed for green lights. How? Affirming statements reduce defensiveness, which helps when you get to tougher issues (what's not going so well). They also build self-esteem and reinforce positive behaviors. Affirmations are not cheerleading, which is more general; they refer to something specific. Highlighting your child's strengths and recognizing positive behaviors will improve your relationship with your child *and* help her to change.

For example, you can:

- Acknowledge effort: "You're really showing some commitment to getting home on time."
- State your appreciation: "I appreciate your openness and honesty today."
- Catch the person doing something right: "Thanks for helping your brother."
- Give a compliment: "I like the way you said that. You really have a way with people."
- Express hope, caring, or support: "I hope this weekend goes well for you!"

3. Reflections – Also called **active listening**, reflections involve restating some or all of what you think the person talking to you said. Your reflection can simply restate the words you heard, or it may reflect the feeling in the words; it can even infer meaning, as long as you are open to maybe getting it wrong! Reflections are statements, not questions (which can slow down or redirect the other person).

As well as communicating that you understand what your child is saying, reflections make sure you actually *do* understand what she is saying—or, if you get it wrong, that you are trying. Reflecting is not necessarily agreeing, but it is being willing to hear how your child sees things, instead of immediately countering. Reflective listening helps a discussion go forward, even or especially after you've hit a red light.

4. Summaries – With open questions, affirmations, and reflections, you may end up in a long and productive conversation! **Summarizing** communicates that you were listening, and helps pull together the important things that were said. It also helps your child to organize her thoughts more coherently if they were jumbled, if you can tie them together in a logical way, and can lead her to connect certain dots. Summaries can even guide the conversation toward a next step, without forcing an agenda. Like reflections, summaries should come with permission for your child to disagree with or correct the record as you recount it. Try to summarize as accurately as possible, without editing the conversation to include what you wished she had said.

Open Questions

Start with words like *How ("How are things going?")* or *What ("What would be most helpful?")*. (Try to avoid *Why* questions, which can prompt your child to justify her negative behaviors.) Open questions can even be a statement, as in, "*Tell me more about that...*" If a question can be answered with one word, such as "yes" or "no," it is a closed question. Closed questions make *you* work harder trying to find the "perfect" question, and they usually do not get you the answer you were looking for. Consider how you have phrased certain questions in the past and try to turn them into open questions.

Closed Questions	Open Questions
Did you drink last night?	How did you manage your drinking last night?
Don't you want to change?	What would be different if you changed your use of _____?
Why did you do that?	Tell me more about that...

Affirmations

Note some ways that your child has tried to explain her behavior in the past; then imagine affirming responses you could use that recognize the behavior you want her to continue.

Situation	Affirming Statement
I tried not to use but it didn't work out last night.	You took a stab at doing something difficult.
I know I didn't tell you until you asked me about it.	I appreciate you talking honestly to me about this now.
I DID try to at least not start drinking until later in the party...	It took some courage to try something different last night.

Reflections

Recall some things your child has said to you about how she feels, and how you have responded in the past. Then try to reconstruct your response to make it reflective. Notice the impulse to "correct" what your child is saying. What you get for your correction is usually further justification by her of her "rightness." What you get for letting her have her version of events is a greater likelihood that she will hear another perspective.

Your Child's Statement	"Counter" Response	"Reflective" Response
You never listen to me.	That's not true, I...	You feel you're not being heard...
I don't want to stop drinking.	Don't you see that you have a problem?!	Alcohol is really important to you.
I didn't use last night.	Yeah, but it's only one night.	Not using was a priority for you last night and you were successful.

The Information Sandwich

Part of parenting is providing information that your child needs to grow up and get along in the world, from reasons to wear a bike helmet and how to open a bank account to what time is curfew, as well as feedback about how things—his behavior, your interactions—are going. In fact, information and feedback figure in any human interchange, not just with your child. The "information sandwich" technique is a three-step process for making information (the contents

of the sandwich) palatable for the other person. By layering information between asking permission and checking back or clarifying after, sandwiching helps the person receive it, take it in, and feel empowered to use it.

1. Asking permission – This conversational equivalent of knocking on the door before you enter has several benefits. First, by asking permission to give them information, you help the other person make a fundamental motivational shift: you allow him to invite you in. Consider your interactions with people: if someone shows up at your house unexpectedly, it's a different proposition than when you have asked for the company. In the latter case, you can prepare and arrange things in a way that is comfortable for you. You can give your child a similar courtesy in conversation.

For example:

- *"Would it be helpful for you to hear about...?"*
- *"Could I offer a thought?"*
- *"Can I ask a question?"*

- *"I have a couple of ideas...but did you want to say your ideas first?"*
- *"Would it be alright if I expressed one concern I have about this plan?"*

Asking permission is one way to make sure the light is green *before* you proceed with the content of your discussion, and it increases the chances that the light *will* be green, as it enhances your child's sense of safety and control. Plus, it honors his independence by giving him a choice. This may seem like a small point, but it can have a profound effect on the conversation when your child feels like he is a participant rather than a passive or reluctant recipient of your words—the difference between talking *at* and talking *with*. This spirit of collaboration is fundamental to motivational therapies, and is equally powerful in conversations. Asking permission increases the likelihood that the other person will hear what follows. One last point: truly asking permission means leaving room for them to say "No, I'd rather not hear this right now." So much better to know this than to speak to deaf ears.

2. Providing information – Permission granted, you would relate the information or feedback in question. Here are a few tips.

- *Provide options.* Whenever possible, it helps to offer more than one good option. It's harder to reject multiple options wholesale, as it puts your child in a position to weigh the pros and cons of each rather than simply say "no."

- *Offer; don't impose.* By the same logic of asking permission, your child will more likely hear, appreciate, and use information that is offered rather than forced on him.

- *Allow disagreement.* As much as possible, leave room for your child to not accept or agree with the information. By asking permission and providing options you better the chances that he will, but it's still his right to disagree. Collaborators don't tell each other what to do; they resolve it together. Allowing for disagreement means the conversation doesn't depend on agreement to go forward or, conversely, come to a screeching halt every time you disagree.

We're not suggesting that you and your child act as equals in all things, with no hierarchy of authority and everybody "just being friends." But to the extent you can allow your child autonomy and stay in communication, you will encounter less defensiveness—in other words, more green lights.

3. Checking back or clarifying – The top layer of the sandwich helps your child process the information and remain open to the discussion. Essentially, you want to know how the information was received: whether your child understood the information or feedback, whether it was digestible or emotionally acceptable—or did he get too mad, hurt, or sad to take in what you said?—and so on. For example:

- *"Does that make sense to you?"*

- *"I just wanted to check back about…"*

- *"I'm not sure I said that very clearly…"*

All together, the sandwich technique is a great way to keep communication open and constructive, offering chances to understand if there is a breakdown, as well as to develop collaboration.

OFFERING INFORMATION WORKSHEET

 Think of a circumstance in which you have information or feedback to give—to your child or to another person in your life — about substance use or anything else. This exercise will show you how to build a permission sandwich around it. Start with the middle, information layer, and consider how the other person might react. Next, write out how you will ask for permission first, and how you will check back after. Then consider how the other person's experience of the information, and his reaction to it, might differ given the sandwich.

Step 1: Write down the information or feedback you would like to give to another person.

I would like to let _____[person's name] know that:

_____.

Step 2: What kind of reaction do you imagine?

_____.

Step 3: Now put the content from Step 1 in a "sandwich":

How will you ask for permission to give them this information?

_____.

How will you check back?

_____.

Step 4: Consider how this interaction might go differently (versus Step 1 alone) using the permission sandwich.

_____.

Remember, you can practice any new skill in lower risk, less difficult situations and relationships first. Then, when you're ready, try it with your child in testier circumstances and see how it goes.

4. COMMUNICATING WITH LOVE: VALIDATING AND EMPATHIZING

 The last two letters of LOVE have less to do with specific strategies and more with the background music of communication: understanding where your child is coming from, or what it's like to walk the world in her shoes (empathy); and acknowledging her experience—her thoughts, feelings, motivations, and perspective—as valid (validation). As we discussed with the use of reflections, you can validate and empathize without endorsing your child's behavior.

Validating

Validating is the simple act of acknowledging another person's experience without needing to qualify it in any way. Adolescents and young adults, especially, need validation as they naturally struggle to define who they are, what they can and cannot do, "who's the boss of them," and how they will manage themselves and their life. Young people with substance problems and related issues can end up with a pervasive sense of feeling invalidated by their parents and others. Assuring a young person that you do not view her as stupid or crazy or delinquent takes a major tinderbox out of the conversation.

Empathizing

Also not a strategy, but a powerful function of communication, empathy is truly feeling "where the other person is coming from"—how she understands her situation, her point of view—and conveying this in some way to your child, often in only a few words ("wow, that seems really scary"; "that would have made me really mad too"). It is a powerful tool in reducing shame and helping your child open up to different ways of thinking about things.

Both empathizing and validating are conveyed through your attitude and approach (respectful, kind, open, and so on) as much as with specific words.

Together, these four aspects of communicating with L-O-V-E will facilitate hearing, being heard, and communicating in a more caring, respectful way with your child as well as in your life. We again suggest practicing as the key to getting better at these skills, and in particular practicing in "easier," less stressful situations, rather than starting with the most important and tension-filled topic you need to discuss with your child.

5. THE 7 ELEMENTS OF POSITIVE COMMUNICATION

In addition to the LOVE communication skills taken from Motivational Interviewing, CRAFT prescribes **positive communication skills** as additional communication tools for your toolbox. You might be thinking: "wouldn't that be nice...to just be positive!" But CRAFT breaks it down into seven elements, all within your reach. These elements will improve any kind of communication, but they are especially useful for *making requests*. What we have found with these seven elements is they are both straightforward *and* difficult to do, so practice is important.

"Positive communication" does not mean only saying nice things and avoiding conflict. Here's what it does mean: (For examples and more explanation, see our chapter on Positive Communication in *Beyond Addiction*.)

1
Be Brief

Most people say more than necessary when they haven't planned it in advance, especially when nervous or angry. Try to hone in on your central request ahead of time, and stick to it. Script, edit, and rehearse what you want to say as concisely as possible. Extraneous words can drown out your core message (as in the "waa waa waa" of Charlie Brown's teacher).

2
Be Specific

Vague requests are easy to ignore or misunderstand, and are often difficult to translate into concrete behavior. In contrast, referring to specific behaviors instead of thoughts or feelings makes change observable, measurable, and reinforceable. For instance, instead of telling your child to "be more responsible," specify a behavior you want to see more of: "On school days, I want you to get up when your alarm goes off."

3

Be Positive

Where "positive" entails describing what you *want*, instead of what you *don't want*. This shifts the framing from critical and complaining to supportive and doable, and ties into positive reinforcement strategies, since it's easier to reward someone for doing something—a concrete, verifiable *thing*—than for not doing something. Being positive in this way decreases defensiveness and rebellion and promotes motivation. Framed positively, "Stop coming home late" becomes "Come home by curfew time."

4

Label Your Feelings

Kept brief and in proportion, a description of your emotional reaction to the problem at hand can help elicit empathy and consideration from your child. For best results, state your feelings in a calm, nonaccusatory manner. If your feelings are very intense, it can be a good strategy to tone them down. So if you were feeling "furious and terrified" you might say "frustrated and worried."

5

Offer An Understanding Statement

The more the other person believes that you "get" why he is acting the way he is, the less defensive he will be and the more likely to hear you and oblige. Plus, trying to understand your child's perspective builds your empathy, which will help the relationship.

6

Take Partial Responsibility

Sharing in a problem, even a tiny piece of the problem, decreases defensiveness and promotes collaboration. It shows your child that you're interested in solving, not blaming. Accepting partial responsibility does not mean taking the blame or admitting fault; it communicates "We're in this together."

7

Offer to Help

Especially when phrased as a question, an offer to help can communicate non-blaming, problem-solving support. Try asking, "Would it help if...?" Or simply, "How can I help?" A little goes a long way to improve communication and generate ideas. ("Yeah, if you texted me a reminder, that would help.")

POSITIVE COMMUNICATION WORKSHEET

 Don't expect fully formed positive communications to spring from your lips spontaneously. Like any new skill, it will probably feel awkward at first. Start by writing down what you want to say. Rehearse, fine-tune, role-play with someone else to see how it goes before you go live. Use this exercise to plan a request you would like to make of your child.

Step 1:
Write out your request, as you'd usually say it.

_____

_____

_____

_____

_____

Step 2:
Now modify your request according to the seven elements of positive communication.

Be Positive. Tell your child what you want him to do rather than what you *don't* want him to do.

First Try:	Modified:
Stop leaving your clothes on the floor.	*Please put your clothes in the hamper.*

Your positive request:

_____

_____

_____

_____

Be Brief. Only one request at a time, and stick to your point. (No: "and another thing...!")

First Try:	Modified:
I want you to do a better job of cleaning up - your room is a mess, and your clothes are everywhere. You're driving me crazy.	I would like you to pick up your clothes.

Your brief, positive request:

_____

_____

_____

_____

Be Specific. Make sure you are clear about your request.

First Try:	Modified:
Just be tidier with your clothes!	Put your clothes in the hamper.

Your specific, brief, positive request:

_____

_____

_____

_____

Label your feelings. Identify a feeling and describe it without being too intense or lengthy. Bonus points for also including a positive feeling.

First Try:	Modified:
It makes me crazy how little you seem to care about things!	I feel frustrated when I come home and see clothes lying around. I'd really appreciate your help in this.

Your feeling(s) labeled:

_____

_____

_____

_____

Offer an understanding statement. Use this strategy to help your child feel heard and non-defensive.

First Try:	Modified:
I'm not asking anything of you that I don't ask of everyone else; we all chip in.	I know you feel rushed to get to your practice and don't think you have time to deal with your clothes.

Your understanding statement:

_____

_____

_____

_____

Take partial responsibility. This is not saying it's your fault, but it's helpful to find a piece of the problem, however small, that you can share.

First Try:	Modified:
It's not my job to be your maid!	I realize I haven't told you how much it bothers me. I can't expect you to read my mind.

Your acceptance of partial responsibility:

_____

_____

_____

_____

_____

Offer to help. See if there is anything you can do to help your child achieve your request.

First Try:	Modified:
You're going to have to grow up sooner or later.	Would it help to have an extra hamper in your room so you don't have to go to the laundry room?

Your offer to help:

_____

_____

_____

_____

_____

Now try putting it all together. You can play with the order and wording to make it sound as natural as possible. Keep in mind that even the most perfectly scripted request won't guarantee the outcome you want. It will, however, increase the odds of being heard.

Tips for practice:

1. Start with small-ticket items that are less important; also start by practicing in the context of safer or easier relationships (practice with your husband or sister instead of your child).

2. You don't need to use all seven steps in every interaction. (Though trying all of them, at least for practice, can help you get the hang of it.)

3. Watch the timing of when you deliver your request. It should not be when your child is under the influence or hung over, and you both should be in reasonably good moods and not rushing off somewhere.

4. Try not to get discouraged if it doesn't go so well the first few, or many, times. It takes effort and practice to get out of negative ruts. We believe—because research shows—it's worth it.

There are classic communication traps you can recognize a mile away… if you know what to look for. Here are some of the most common.

The Information Trap: *If only he knew the facts he would see things differently and change.* Information can be helpful, especially when it fills a gap. It is less helpful to tell your child something he already knows. When you do have fresh information, offering it in a "sandwich" as you learned in Section 3 will maximize the chances that it gets across. But there are no magic words for change, so try to be patient. Improving the quality of your communication over time will help, as well as being a valuable change in and of itself.

The Lecture Trap: This is a deeper information trap. One sign that you have entered this trap is when you find yourself talking "at" your child about what you think he should do, what his problems are, what went wrong last week, and so on, rather than talking "with" him.

The Labeling Trap: Labels are not necessary for change, and at times get in the way. This trap results in a conversation being about labels and not behavior ("You're an addict." —"No, I'm not").

The Blaming Trap: When you're worried, frustrated, or sad about a situation, it is easy to get stuck in the blaming trap—who is at fault or who is to blame? This trap shuts down a conversation and backs your child's motivation into a corner.

The Taking-Sides Trap: If you take *only one side* of a discussion, it's practically a set up for your child to take the other, and she may end up defending behaviors she actually feels ambivalent about. Instead of one side against the other you can be on the same side, the side of constructive conversation, considering different options together.

The Question-and-Answer Trap: <u>Closed questions</u> set off this trap and result in an interview, or worse, an interrogation ("Did you get high last night? Did you forget your phone? Did you do your homework?"). Open questions are more likely to steer your conversation to a productive exchange.

HELPING

This section will cover a variety of critical tools for encouraging change in your child's behavior and motivation. They follow "Taking Care of Yourself" and "Communicating" because those are the foundations of sustaining change and keeping things on track day-to-day. The tools in this section will help you understand motivation and how it is different for different people, how to reinforce new and positive behaviors as well as how to deal with negative behaviors, how to understand and allow for ambivalence in your child (and the sometimes jagged upward course of change), and very importantly, paying attention to collaboration with your co-parent.

This section includes seven topics:

1 One Answer Does Not Fit All

2 Parent Collaboration
Parent Collaboration Worksheet

3 Behaviors Make Sense... Even Your Child's
Behaviors Make Sense Worksheet

4 Reinforcement: Your Love Matters
Reinforcement Worksheet

5 Natural Consequences: Allowing Them to Happen
Natural Consequences Worksheet

6 Your Consequences: Making Them Happen
Your Consequences Worksheet

7 Warning! Ambivalence Is Normal

1. ONE ANSWER DOES NOT FIT ALL

"What should I do if my teenager is drinking or using drugs?" The answer is that there are many answers, many paths, and many ways to help your child change his relationship to substances. The answer for your child will depend on the dynamics of your family as a whole and your child as a unique individual. It will depend on what sorts of other problems he has, how long the behavior has been going on, his age, who his friends are and what they think about substances, and about fifty other things. One size does not fit all. There are as many ways to change, as there are children. It's a more complicated, perhaps unsettling answer than a universal solution, but worth grappling with because it's reality.

Improving family relations and friendships, reinforcing healthy habits, and introducing new interests, all help. Treatment and other therapeutic activities can help, and there are many options—some better supported by evidence than others, some more available and affordable than others, but altogether many possibilities to explore. In other words, many ways your child can get the help he needs.

If you are brave enough to ask for it, or probably even if you don't ask, people will give you their opinions, advice, and even veiled criticism about helping your child. You might hear, "How could you let that happen in your own house? You should kick him out!" in one ear, and "We don't get worked up about things like that—after all, think what we all managed to live through! Parents are over-protective these days," in the other.

Whom should you listen to? What's the best advice? Again, no one size fits all **and** having a choice among treatment plans and plans for change in general predicts positive outcomes. *On these points the evidence is crystal clear*. Giving people options helps them feel less trapped and invites them to get invested in the plan. This is also true for your child.

So, as you think through ways to help your child, do your homework. If the first (or fifth) person you consult tells you they know exactly what you should do, you might want to get some more opinions, especially if the person says this without meeting your child. Black-and-white thinking abounds when it comes to figuring out how to deal with a substance use problem, and you may hear the range from "You have to deal with this now or he'll be an addict for life" to "It's just a little pot and he will grow out of it." Falling into the black-and-white thinking trap can prevent you from understanding the subtleties of who your child really is and how to help him. Give yourself permission to take the time you need to sort out what is going on and understand your options and try to be patient—with yourself, your partner, and your child.

After you collect information about your situation, we encourage you to trust *your* sense of what is best, putting aside your feelings of guilt and self-doubt.   Getting input is important, but you also need to trust what you know about your child and your family.

> **A Suggestion:** If you consider taking your child for a professional assessment, it may be helpful to describe it to him as a "consultation," which sounds less like "trapped in therapy forever." Ask around. Ask people you know about psychiatrists, psychologists, social workers, and so on that they liked. "The Top 100 Doctors" may not be the best place to start; the guy your nephew liked might be a more appealing and accessible port in the storm.

The Parent's 20 Minute Guide

ONE ANSWER DOES NOT FIT ALL: WORKSHEET

 This week, make a list of all the advice you get from other people about how to deal with your child's substance use. Make note of the advice that triggers feelings or thoughts of self-doubt in you. Next to each one of those "triggers," list a potential alternative thought or coping response. This is an exercise in trusting yourself and practicing sifting through the feedback you'll get out in the world...

Trigger Comment	Alternative thought/Coping Response
"You should send him away to rehab."	We don't think he needs that intensive a treatment, and we want to help him make changes in the context of his normal life.
"You should kick him out."	We're not willing to kick him out right now we can think of many steps to try before taking such drastic action.
"You should chill out. It's just pot."	We are concerned because of the changes we see: grades dropping, different friends, quitting basketball, apathetic about things he used to care about.

2. PARENT COLLABORATION

When a child struggles with substance or other behavior problems, communication often breaks down *between the adults* who love that child.* Most people struggle to not get defensive or lose their cool in situations they don't understand or know how to control, and it's not uncommon for parents to feel at wits' end *with each other* when their child is doing risky, upsetting things. Disagreements are understandable. After all, misalignment can easily happen in the best of circumstances over lower-stakes issues like bedtime and vegetables; the more serious the issue, the more polarizing it can be. But helping depends in no small part on finding a way to collaborate with your co-parent (and anyone else involved in raising your child).

As you try to help your child change their relationship with substances, it will be important for every adult involved to give clear directions and consistent consequences (positive and negative). Change, even change for the better, is difficult and your child will feel ambivalent about it. It will be hard for her to make different friends, or not be high at parties, or leave earlier than other kids. The more ambivalent she is, the more important it is for you to make your expectations clear. Different expectations (explicit or implied) between you and your partner amount to mixed messages for your child.

Additionally, the more agreement you can reach with your partner, the less stressed you will each feel and the happier you will both be. And with less conflict and stress in general you can, in turn, be more positive with your child.

Alignment and collaboration with your partner doesn't mean across-the-board, united-front agreement on "the party line," especially with older children. Children over sixteen live in the adult world enough to know that uniform agreement is not realistic. Alignment can mean understanding what you agree on, what you don't agree on, and what the "policy" is in any case ("Your father and I have a somewhat different feeling about this, but we've decided it's important for you to be home by midnight"). You can acknowledge differences and still align your expectations.

---

* These issues can be more acute for parents who are separated, divorced, or otherwise living in different locations. More effort may be required on everyone's part to overcome a history of differences, communicate effectively, and cooperate with the skills.

PARENT COLLABORATION WORKSHEET

 Problem-solve misalignment between you and your partner or co-parent. How, specifically, might you improve communication and reduce tension? See each other's perspectives? Consider taking time out from discussing problems (or talk about things that are going well!), as well as scheduling uninterrupted time to strategize about the challenges you share. Start small, and try to manage your expectations... it may take many steps and a lot of practice to get in alignment. Keeping in mind the overall goal of goodwill between the two of you in order to help your child and yourselves, set doable goals you can measure, and monitor the natural drift back into familiar roles and patterns.

Step 1: Brainstorm ways you could improve communication and collaboration with your partner or co-parent. Don't rule out any ideas at first glance, even if you are not ready to try them yet. Consider the pros and cons of each idea, and see if you'd be willing to try it. Make one your goal for this week.

Collaboration idea: *We (husband and I) will find 10 (full) minutes a day to talk about plans for the next day.*

Pros:	Cons:
1. *We will be less likely to get our wires crossed about who is doing what.* 2. *I won't worry all day.*	*I feel so busy and he gets mad at me when I say we need to talk.*

<u>Communication idea</u>: *I will practice active listening 3 times this week by asking him how his day was and listening for 3 (full) minutes while he answers.*

Pros:	Cons:
1. My husband will feel appreciated by me.	At that time of night I am frantic and I may not be able to do it, which will make me feel like a failure.
2. It will force me to slow down and be calmer.	

<u>Your collaboration idea</u>:

Pros:	Cons:

<u>Your communication idea</u>:

Pros:	Cons:

Step 2: Do the same for reducing tension between you. Brainstorm, consider the pros and cons of each idea, and choose one to try this week.

<u>Tension-reducing idea</u>: *I will agree to try one of my husband's ideas for a consequence for our daughter when she comes home late, even if it's not one I would choose myself.*

Pros:	Cons:
My husband will feel less defensive, like I shoot down everything he says. Maybe he will also be more open to my thoughts.	*I think some of his ideas are too harsh and I won't want to agree to them no matter what.*

<u>Your tension-reducing ideas</u>:

Pros:	Cons:

Step 3: When you have selected communication, collaboration, and tension-reducing goals for this week, list potential obstacles that come to mind. Then, think of coping skills you could use to maximize your chances of getting around each obstacle and reaching your goal(s).

Obstacle	Coping Skill
He works late every night this week and will be too tired to want to talk about how to manage our daughter.	I will ask him to get up 20 minutes early so we can talk before he goes to work. And I'll promise to make him coffee.

The Parent's 20 Minute Guide

3. BEHAVIORS MAKE SENSE...
EVEN YOUR CHILD'S

If your child is using drugs or alcohol, it's unlikely that they are simply being a "bad kid" or *trying* to drive you crazy (although it feels like it). His behavior (in this case substance use) is rewarding in some way – emotionally, physically, socially, perhaps all of the above. In psychology we call this "reinforcement," and it applies to motivation and change in all of us. People take action—work hard at a job, study for a test, smoke pot—and repeat that action because they get something from doing it. Getting a raise, doing well on a test, or being the life of the party is the reward or "reinforcer" for the action, the reason they keep doing it. Generally, people do not persist in a behavior (for very long) unless it affords some benefit.

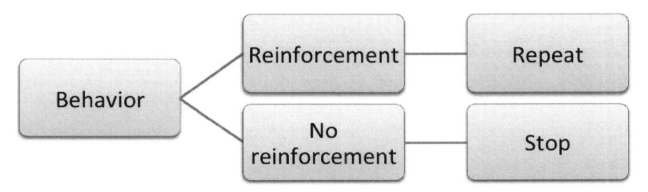

Feeling relaxed, exhilarated, less anxious, braver, funnier, and part of the group, are all potential *benefits* of using substances. If there were no benefits, there would be no use. This is important because knowing what, in particular, your child gets from using substances provides clues about *what could happen instead*. For example, if you think that your child is drinking in part because it helps him take a break from his hectic school schedule, you can come up with other, healthy ways he might be able to get those breaks. You might decide to schedule "homework-free" time or relax some of the pressure you notice he's feeling at home.

Understanding what your child gets from using can also lower your fear and anxiety, as it makes the behavior less random and more predictable. If he uses to fit in with other kids, then you know he's more at risk when he's out socializing than home with the family. Knowing this won't eliminate your anxiety completely, but it can reduce it. And as you learn CRAFT strategies, you will be equipped to intervene constructively to influence the patterns.

Finally, understanding your child's reinforcers will help you empathize with him. Why would you want to empathize with such destructive behavior? It will help you take it less personally (as in, "How can he do this to us?!"), and feel less angry and more connected, which will give you energy for helping him change. Instead of thinking he is irresponsible or torturing you, you can see the underlying loneliness, insecurity, depression, or boredom, which are all things you can help your child address. In turn, and even more important, understanding your child's behavior instead of just being upset about it can help *him* feel understood, which will make him more likely to collaborate on a plan for change.

BEHAVIORS MAKE SENSE...
WORKSHEET

 In order to promote positive activities that can compete with your child's use of substances, you'll need to understand what is reinforcing for him about his use. In this exercise, we ask you to brainstorm what your child may like about using substances. If this is distressing, bear in mind, his reasons to use are clues pointing towards reasons to do something else instead. If you're still not convinced of the value of this exercise, or you just need a break from it, you may want to read the chapter on motivation in our book, *Beyond Addiction*.

Step 1: List any reasons why your child may be using substances. Start with reasons s/he has told you in the past ("It's fun," "everyone smokes pot," etc.) and also include reasons you believe from your own observations. Try to avoid blaming or accusatory reasons ("because he's an idiot," "because he doesn't care about anything," "he's trying to piss me off.")	**Step 2**: Outline the basic needs that each reason in Step 1 fulfills. Below is a list of potential needs, and you can add others.	**Step 3**: Once you have identified underlying reasons why your child might be using substances, brainstorm alternative ways you could help him/her to address that issue.
	Stress reduction Anxiety relief Enjoyment Social interaction Mood stabilizing Risk taking or thrill Rebellion _____ _____ _____ _____ _____ _____ _____ _____ _____	

Reasons for Use	**Basic Needs Being Met**	**Alternatives**
"Everyone else is smoking pot."	Social comfort, maybe anxiety relief.	Talk to doctor about anxiety; help expose him to new groups of friends.
"I just need to chill out."	Stress reduction.	Give time to unwind after school without chores.
"It's more fun when I'm high."	Enjoyment, maybe social interactions and comfort, maybe thrill seeking.	Discuss the pros and the cons of using.

Reasons for Use	Basic Needs Being Met	Alternatives

4. REINFORCEMENT: YOUR LOVE MATTERS

Since you now know that "your child's behavior makes sense" because substance use is reinforcing, we can move on to positive reinforcement as one of the core helping strategies in CRAFT. That is, you can use the same behavioral mechanisms that reinforce substance use to reinforce other behaviors instead. Basically, reward your child when she does something that you want her to do again (coming home sober, picking up her room, talking in a calm manner, being nice to her sister). A reward can be a compliment, a hug, a favorite meal, a gift card, or—and this is often overlooked—simply acknowledging what she has done. Linked to a behavior, such "gold stars" help your child start to see the value in acting that way again. Your part is to figure out what's rewarding to her and tolerate the discomfort you may feel in rewarding behavior you think she "should be doing anyway."

Is reinforcement bribery?

How will your child learn to want change herself if she is "just" doing it for the reward?

In fact, positive reinforcement, when practiced consistently, helps your child's internal motivation. Why? Because with practice, over time, she will experience the benefits of the new behavior and it will become rewarding in and of itself. Meanwhile, your reinforcement boosts her willingness to engage in new behaviors in the first place, so that she can start experiencing the intrinsic benefits of positive change.

How Will Reinforcing Change Anything?

The value in reinforcing positive behavior by rewarding it is that it can start to compete with the reinforcing effects of drugs and alcohol. In essence, your child can learn to "feel good" in other ways rather than using drugs/alcohol. They can feel proud of themselves, acknowledged, recognized for their efforts. All the feel good things that contribute to a healthy self-esteem and ability to cope with life.

What Might be Happening Instead?

Contrary to what you might have heard, confrontation and punishment are not the most helpful strategies to use when you are trying to encourage change. In fact, they are likely to push things in the exact opposite direction as your child acts to defend their position. Nor is detaching the answer, because it leaves you with no way to positively influence your child. It may also be that your child's *un*healthy behavior gets most if not all of your attention, even at times when she isn't using—because you're still fuming after the last time, or worried about the next. When a family is caught in a cycle of confrontation and punishment, negative attention may be the only kind the child receives.

While your negative feelings are understandable, they can prevent you from noticing the good things that also happen (when she's sober and doing her homework, sober and having dinner with the family, and so on). It may seem to your child that she can't do anything right (because you are upset all the time), so why bother? The key to your child making changes that stick will be your attention (which is a reward in and of itself) to the healthy, adaptive behaviors that you see. Reward your child when she is not using! In other words, "catch her being good" (as rare as that may seem sometimes!). Staying involved and rewarding steps towards healthy behavior is what will work to help motivate your child.

Take a moment to think about meaningful rewards for your child. Here are a few guidelines:

- **Rewards are in the eye of the beholder.**

  A vacation in Italy might feel like winning the lottery to you, but for a child, earning a later curfew and a gift card for music might hit closer to the mark. Spend some time thinking, talking to your partner, or talking to your child about what she finds rewarding. You can also look around for what rewards she is already getting that you might want to tie to her behavior.

- **Rewards fit your child's needs in her current life stage; these may change as she develops.**

  For example, most ten-year-olds prize quality time with a parent, but at seventeen... not so much. Again: rewards are in the eye of the beholder.

- **Rewards follow closely the behavior they're meant to reward.**

  Timing helps link the reward to the behavior, so plan rewards that you can deliver immediately or shortly after (not before) the behavior takes place. Resist the temptation to give something now in the hopes that her behavior will change later.

- **Rewards are things you're willing and able to give.**

  Make sure you're comfortable with the cost and other qualities of the rewards you choose. The new Grand Theft Auto game might be something he'd really like, but if it's not compatible with your values and budget, you can think of something else. Some of the most effective rewards, like your attention, compliments, and affection, are free.

For more guidelines and examples of reinforcement in action, see our whole chapter about it in *Beyond Addiction*.

Practiced consistently over time, positive reinforcement will enhance your child's motivation to change. Try to have patience and don't give up if her behavior doesn't change as fast as you'd like it to. Change takes time. If you're uncertain or find yourself thinking "this doesn't work for my child" or "he doesn't care about anything," review the guidelines: Is the reward rewarding to your child? How's your timing? And bear in mind, consistent behavior change is hard for everyone, but especially for teens and young adults, who are so in flux anyway. Try to tolerate the process and remember that changing behavior patterns takes willingness to resist engaging in them long enough to learn new ones. It's a lot of work!

REINFORCEMENT: WORKSHEET

Reinforcement requires noticing when your child is sober and doing something you like, and rewarding it. This not only increases the likelihood that she'll repeat the wanted behavior, it also contributes to a general sense that her world when she's sober is more rewarding than her world when she's using.

Note: It is NOT reinforcing if you give rewards BEFORE the behavior happens... so resist the temptation to give something NOW in the hopes that their behavior will change LATER.

Step 1: List behaviors you hope will change, and identify a specific, alternative, healthy behavior you would be willing to support for each of them.

Behavior to Change	Alternative Behavior to Reinforce
Coming home after school late and stoned.	Coming home on time and sober.
Getting up late and making the morning stressful for everyone.	Getting up on time.

Example: The behavior I will reward this week:

Coming home from school on time. It's a step towards other behaviors like coming home sober.

The behavior I will reward this week:

Step 2: Brainstorm possible rewards for the healthy behavior. Make sure some of them are free.

Free Rewards	Rewards that Cost Something
If she comes home on time, I will compliment her effort to come home instead of hanging out with her friends.	If she comes home on time I will give her a $5 gift card to download apps.
I will let her play video games for half an hour before doing her homework.	If she comes home on time 5 days in a row, I will drive her to hang out with her friends on Saturday.

The rewards I will give *after* she does the behavior I want to see:

1.

2.

3.

The power of positive reinforcement for positive behavior - finding ways to acknowledge your child's moves in the right direction - is made all the more effective by how you address your child's negative behaviors. The bottom line? Let the negative consequences resulting from "negative" behavior be felt and heard. It may surprise you to learn that the direct, negative outcomes of your child's actions (failed grades, missed social events, a cold supper)—what we call "natural consequences"—are among the most powerful promoters of change.

Many parents have a variety of strategies for meting out punishment for negative behavior (grounding, time outs, withdrawing financial support, scolding) but find it difficult to let the natural consequences happen. You want to protect your child from the effects of neglecting homework or sleeping late. From a behavioral standpoint, however, when you shield your child from the uncomfortable result of his actions, he learns that there's no downside. The net result? Why *wouldn't* he continue the negative behaviors?

Of course, some consequences are too harmful to allow. Your job is to identify the negative consequences you can tolerate and let them "speak for themselves"; they will often be more convincing than anything you could say or do, and you will be relieved of the burden of arguing. The world is a powerful teacher if we let it be.

The combination of reinforcing positive behaviors and allowing the natural consequences of negative behaviors is more powerful than either strategy alone. With this "reinforcement," your child will experience for himself the connection between positive behavior and good things happening, and start to recognize his role as the producer of good (or bad) things in his life.

What is "Enabling?"

It's important to understand this often misused word. It means softening or removing the negative consequences of another person's negative behavior, which in effect *encourages* the continuation of that behavior. If you rush to get your kid out of bed for football practice, even though he stayed out too late the night before, he never has to face his upset coach or teammates. He never has to link his behavioral choice (staying out too late) with the natural consequence (upset coach). He only has to face your upset and stress, which are likely very common and easily tuned out.

The confusion? Many parents think enabling means doing *anything* nice for their child who is abusing substances. If, in your anger and disappointment at certain negative behaviors (using drugs, coming home late), you withdraw *all* your positive attention (even when he is sober and trying to engage in a nice conversation), you create a negative environment that is not good for anyone, you or your child. Making a difference requires understanding the difference:

- **Promote positive behaviors with positive outcomes.**

- **Allow negative behaviors to have negative outcomes.**

Simple, but hard to do. Keep practicing; you'll get better at it, and so will your child.

ALLOWING CONSEQUENCES: WORKSHEET

 This exercise will help you identify specific negative consequences of your child's substance use, the ways you may be intervening to protect him from them, and ways you could allow them to happen.

Step 1: What are the potential or actual natural consequences of your child's substance use? Focus on the "safe to allow" consequences.	Step 2: Is there anything buffering her direct experience of these consequences? Is there anything you are doing, inadvertently or purposefully, to soften these downsides?	Step 3: What can you do to let your child experience one or more natural consequences more directly (without putting her at too much risk)?
Incomplete homework assignments and teachers threatening summer school	Monitoring if assignments are complete	Let her face teachers and have to complete summer school instead of go to camp.
Staying up late and sleeping in, missing soccer practice	Getting her up and driving fast to practice so she doesn't miss it	Let her miss practice and bring her to talk with coach afterwards.
Coming home late and missing dinner	Cooking her a late dinner so she isn't hungry	Let her figure out what to eat on her own.

6. YOUR CONSEQUENCES: MAKING THEM HAPPEN

As a parent, there are times when you need and want to *provide* a negative consequence for unwanted behavior. At these times, clarity and consistency are the keys.

> **Tip:**
>
> Do not use your "biggest hammer" right away. The consequence should fit the behavior, and there should be room for improvement—if you kick him out of the house at the first sign of negative behavior, you won't know whether smaller consequences (coupled with rewards for positive behavior, of course) could have influenced change.
>
> Save the big consequences for the really big stuff, and have some smaller consequences for smaller issues. Even more important, don't threaten any consequence unless you are willing to implement it (don't threaten to kick them out unless you are ready to change your locks).

Clarity – Let your child know *beforehand* what will happen if she engages in the behavior you want her to avoid. This means being clear yourself: figuring out ahead of time realistic and meaningful consequences for the range of behaviors you want to address. (The consequence should match the severity of the behavior, and it must be possible and practical to enforce.) Communicating the plan in advance puts the choice in your child's hands—she knows going in the consequences of acting one way versus another.

Consistency – Everyone involved must be willing to enact the consequence and able to enforce it, as together you should present a united front (even if you feel somewhat differently). Discuss in advance and pick consequences you can agree to and can help each other enforce. For example, if you plan to take away driving privileges for a week if your child comes home drunk, work out who is going to drive her to school and other places she needs to go. If one of you thinks you might waver in following through, then plan how to help each other stay consistent. Communicate at every stage.

Through planning ahead you'll be able to work around obstacles ahead of time. This will help enormously with your consistency. And consistency helps your credibility, your sense of control, and your child's motivation.

Note: It's better not to have any consequences or rewards at all than to promise them to your child and then not follow through. Failing to be consistent hurts your credibility as well as your ability to influence positive change for your child.

YOUR CONSEQUENCES WORKSHEET

 This worksheet is designed to help you establish a consequence for negative behavior as clearly and consistently as possible.

Step 1: In the left-hand column, list your expectations for your child's behavior. Then in the right-hand column, describe the consequence that will result from going against this expectation.

Expectation	Consequence
She will come home on time from the party.	If she is more than 15 minutes late she will not be allowed to use the car the following weekend.

Step 2: Choose one of the above, and plan how you will communicate (in advance) your expectation and consequence to your child. Use your new communication skills.

Example: *I know it is hard to leave your friends, but you need to be home by curfew. If you are more than 15 minutes late you will not be able to use the car next weekend. I'm happy to send a text reminder, if that would help?*

Your communication:

Step 3: Anticipate any obstacle(s) that might get in the way of consistently following through, and plan how you will deal with it.

Example: *I will be working and she may need to get to her soccer game. I will make sure my husband can drive her.*

Your obstacle(s) and solution(s):

7. WARNING!
AMBIVALENCE IS NORMAL

Sometimes change will make sense to your child, other times it won't. He may give reasons for change one day (green lights); and the next day he argues against it (red lights). This motivational seesaw is normal, it's how ambivalence gets expressed and par for the course of virtually any kind of change — from dieting to ending relationships to changing careers — not just changing substance use.

Why might your child feel ambivalent, when the costs seem so clear to you? The change you hope for may have its benefits, but remember, your child gets something from using substances (it's reinforcing!). As a result, sometimes using or not changing makes sense. Changing that behavior requires learning a new behavior to replace it, and the work involved in learning can be hard and uncomfortable.

Change can be understood as a cost-benefit equation, as illustrated by the (less loaded) example below:

Reasons to Exercise/Change (Benefits)	Reasons to Not Exercise/Not Change (Costs)
• Better health	• Feel really awkward in the gym socially
• Increased energy	• Like extra time at home
• Doctor will be happy	• Get fatigued from exercise
• Feel better about myself	• Reminds me how out of shape I am
	• Don't want to pay for gym

This is ambivalence: wanting to go in two directions at the same time, often with good (or good enough) reasons either way. If you listen carefully, you can hear your child's ambivalence in the way he talks about his experiences and decisions. Try to appreciate that his reasons for both changing a behavior and not changing it are reasonable—and don't take the bait! Arguing with ambivalence or trying to make him see your side is just begging for him to defend his reasons for not changing. If you react to "I don't want to change" (red light talk) by arguing, trying to shout it down, or lecturing ("what do you mean you don't want to stop, you are failing school because of it!"), you are probably going to get a defensive response (yelling back or better yet door slamming).   And, you may miss hearing the other more subtle examples of your child's desire to change ("I don't want to have to go to summer school").

Not getting into an argument gives him room to reflect on his own reasons to change. Instead of fighting with ambivalence, you can gently guide his behavior with your responses. You can choose to respond with communication and behavioral strategies that help tip the scale toward change. Patience can come in very handy!

Made in the USA
Lexington, KY
07 August 2016